www.DyslexiaGames.com

Copyright © 2011 the Thinking Tree, LLC
All rights reserved.

Dyslexia Games Series B – Book 2
Friendly Copyright Notice:

ALL DYSLEXIA GAMES, WORKSHEETS, AND MATERIALS MAY <u>NOT</u> BE SHARED, COPIED, EMAILED, OR OTHERWISE DISTRIBUTED TO ANYONE OUTSIDE YOUR HOUSEHOLD OR IMMEDIATE FAMILY (SHARING IS STEALING).

Please refer people interested in Dyslexia Games to our website to purchase their own copy of the materials.

The Thinking Tree LLC • 617 N Swope St. • Greenfield, IN 46140 • info@dyslexiagames.com • +1 (317) 622-8852

I.Q. Challenge

Mind Games, Puzzles & Mysteries

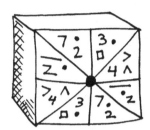 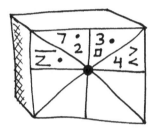 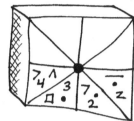

By Sarah J. Brown

Parent Teacher Instructions:

Provide the student with a fine point black pen. The main point of each game is to complete the pattern, drawing or puzzle by filling in the missing parts. The challenge is to figure out what's missing. The games tap into the child's natural problem solving abilities, so he may not need much assistance.

These exercises develop problem solving skills, concentration, intelligence, logic, tracking skills, math skills, memory skills, while tapping into the creative area of the child's mind.

Name:_____ Date:_____

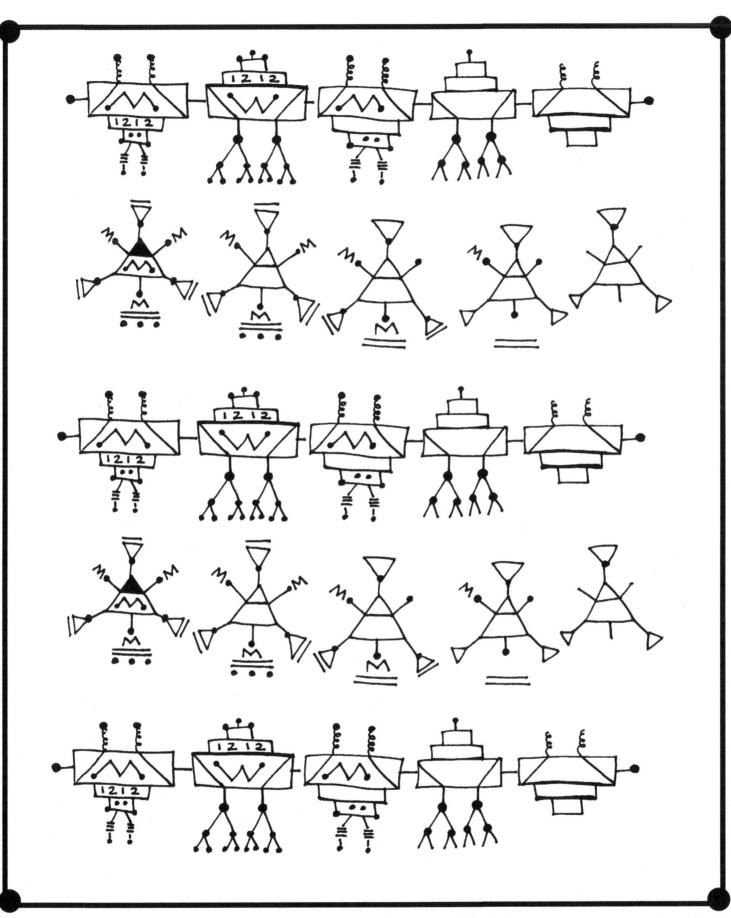

Name:_____ Date:_____

© 2011 all rights reserved. The Thinking Tree, LLC

Name:_____ Date:_____

Name:_____ Date:_____

© 2011 all rights reserved. The Thinking Tree, LLC

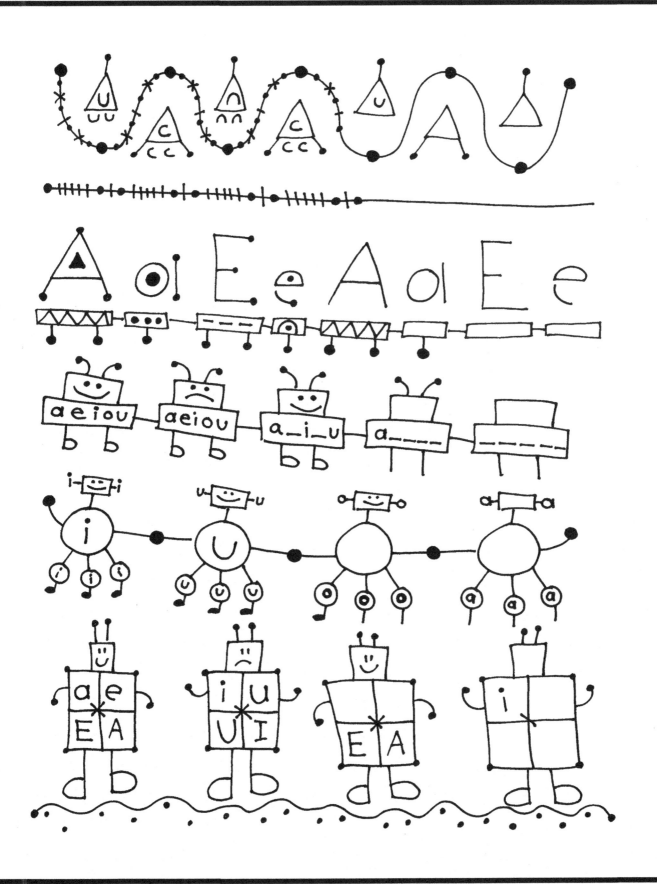

Name:_____ Date:_____

© 2011 all rights reserved. The Thinking Tree, LLC

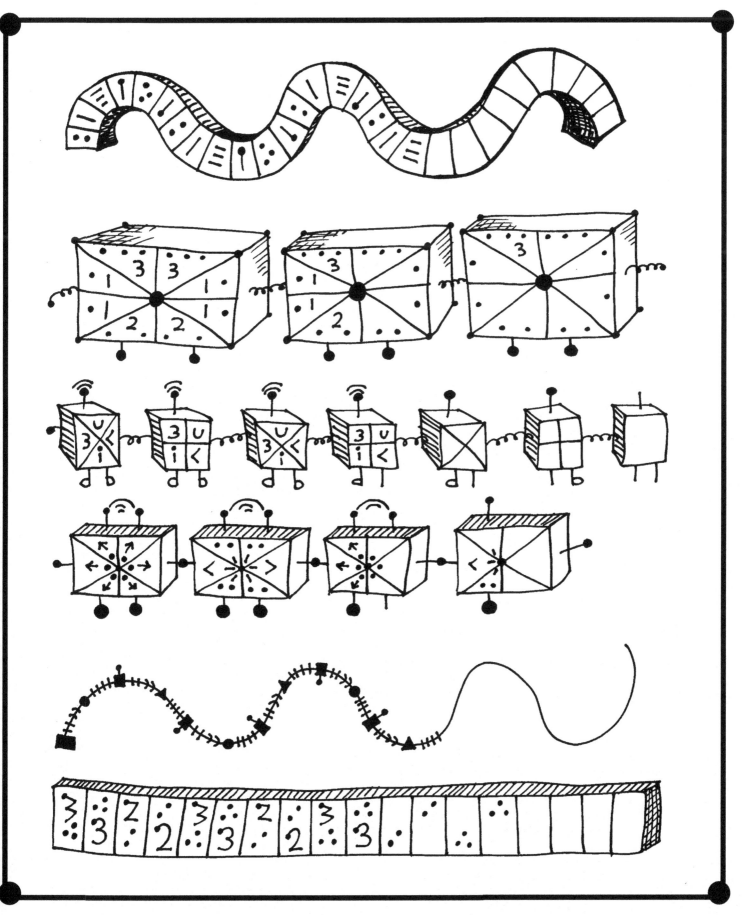

Name:_____ Date:_____

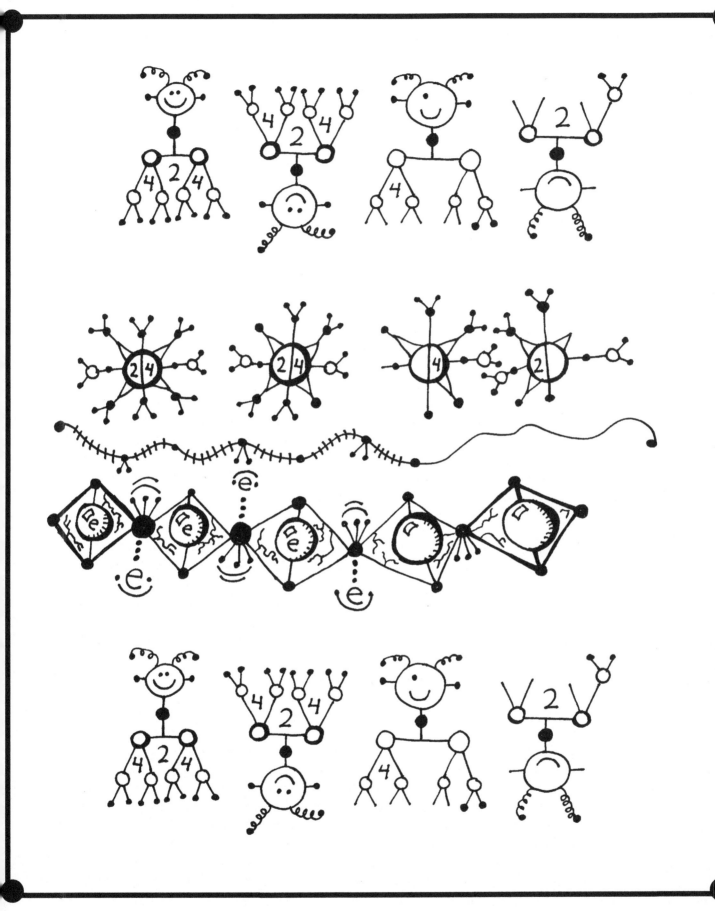

Name:_____ Date:_____

© 2011 all rights reserved. The Thinking Tree, LLC

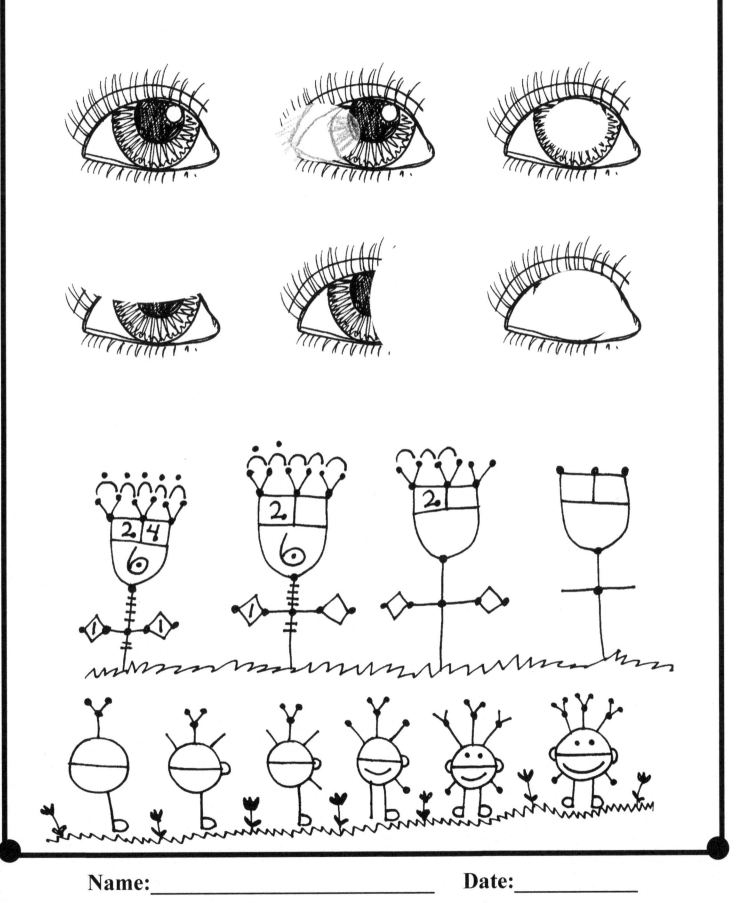

Name:_____ Date:_____

© 2011 all rights reserved. The Thinking Tree, LLC

Name:_____ Date:_____

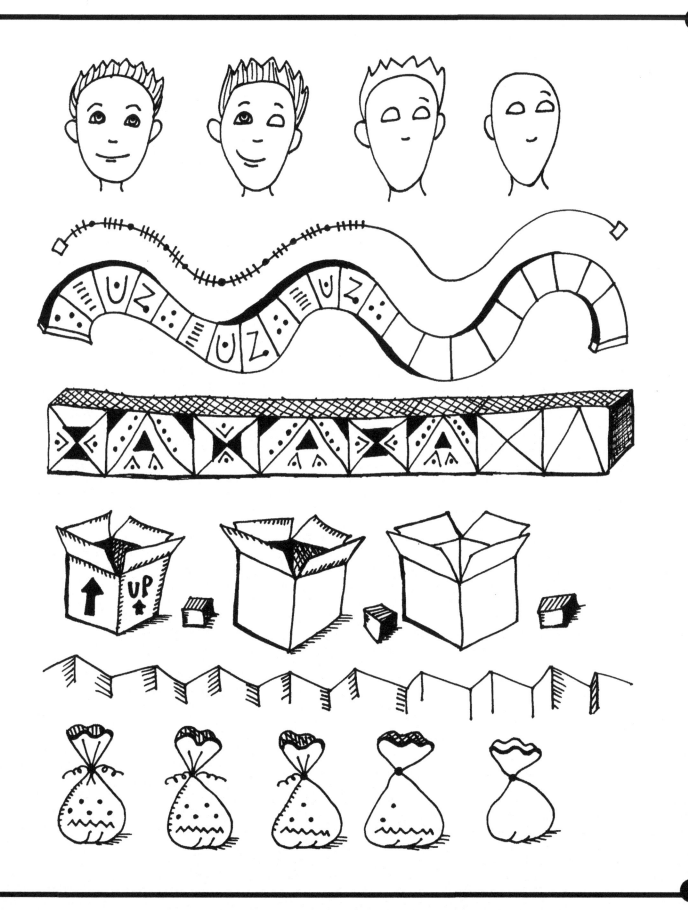

Name:_____ Date:_____

© 2011 all rights reserved. The Thinking Tree, LLC

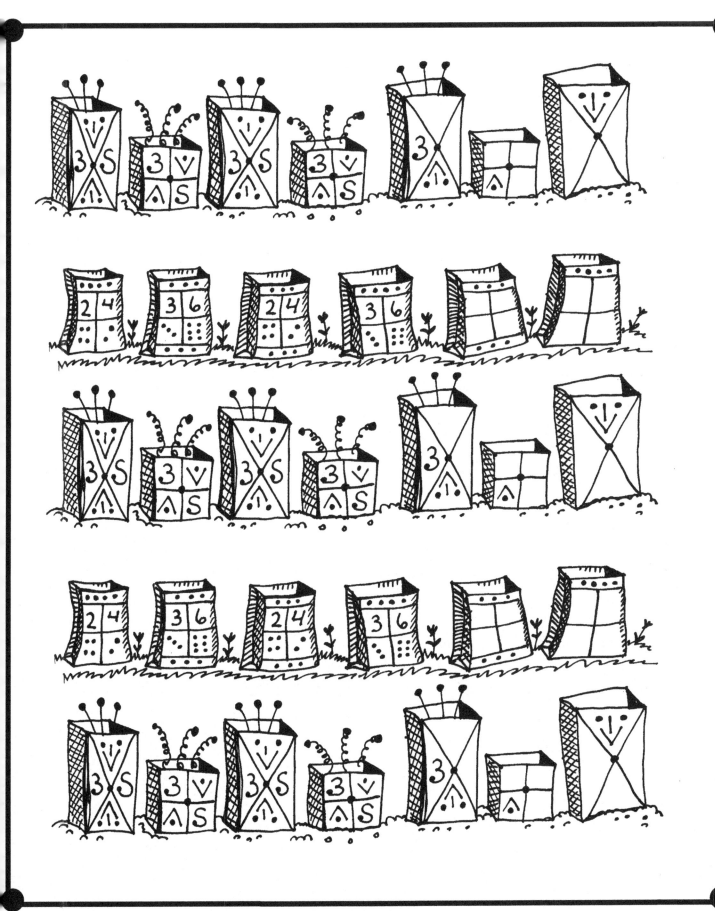

Name:_____ Date:_____

© 2011 all rights reserved. The Thinking Tree, LLC

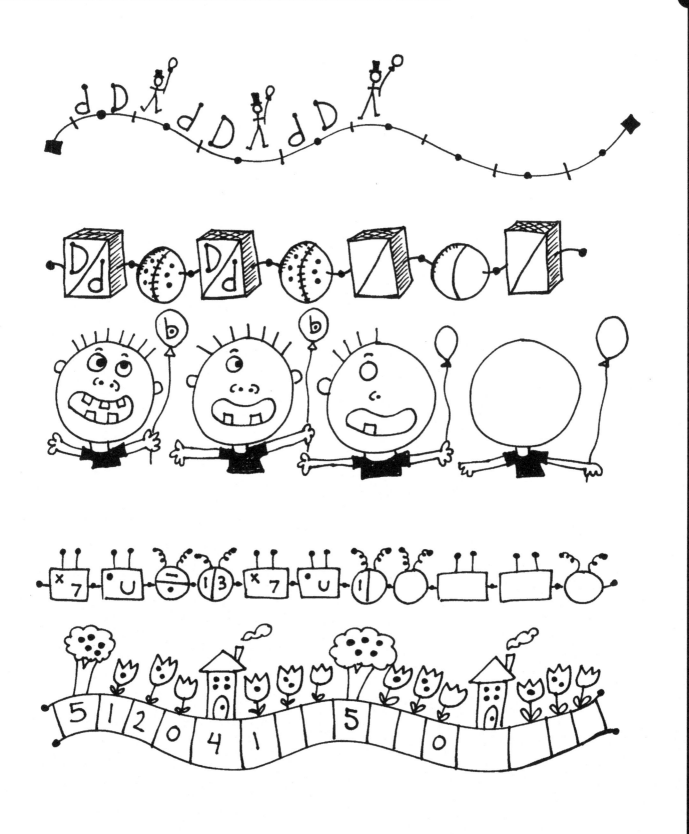

Name:_____ Date:_____

© 2011 all rights reserved. The Thinking Tree, LLC

Name:_____ Date:_____

© 2011 all rights reserved. The Thinking Tree, LLC

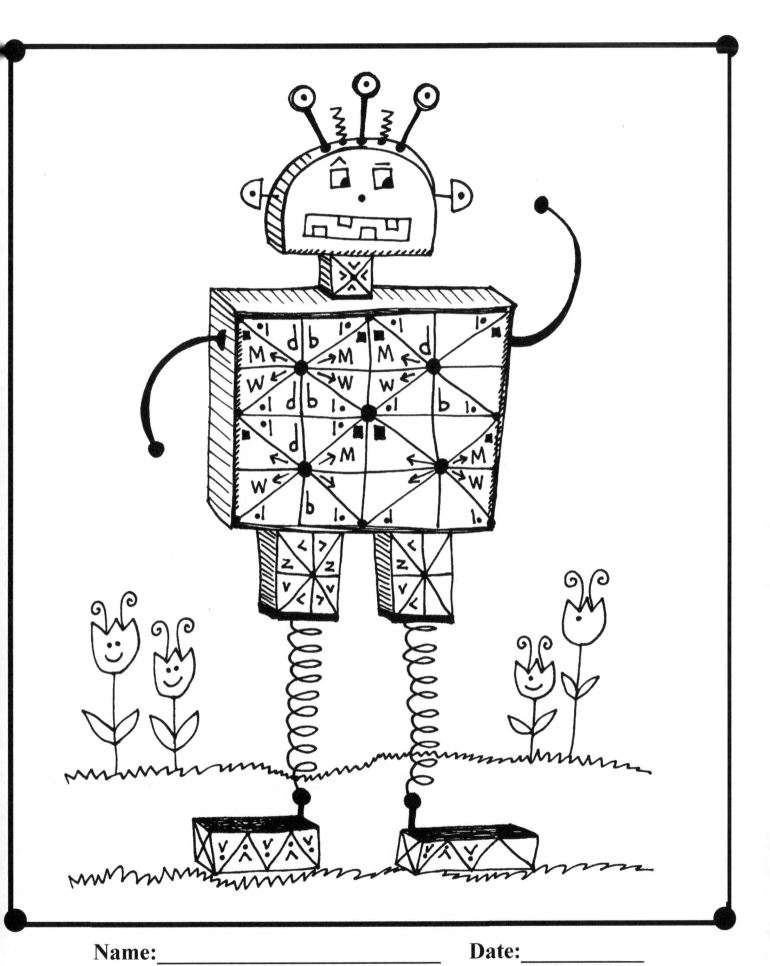

Name:_____ Date:_____

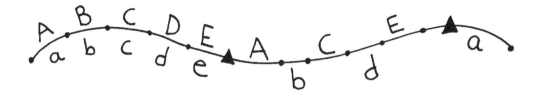

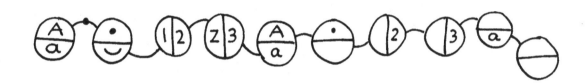

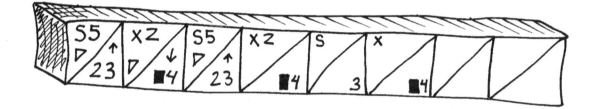

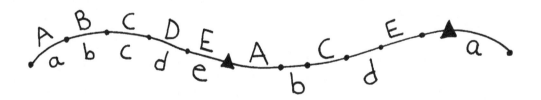

Name:_____   Date:_____

© 2011 all rights reserved. The Thinking Tree, LLC

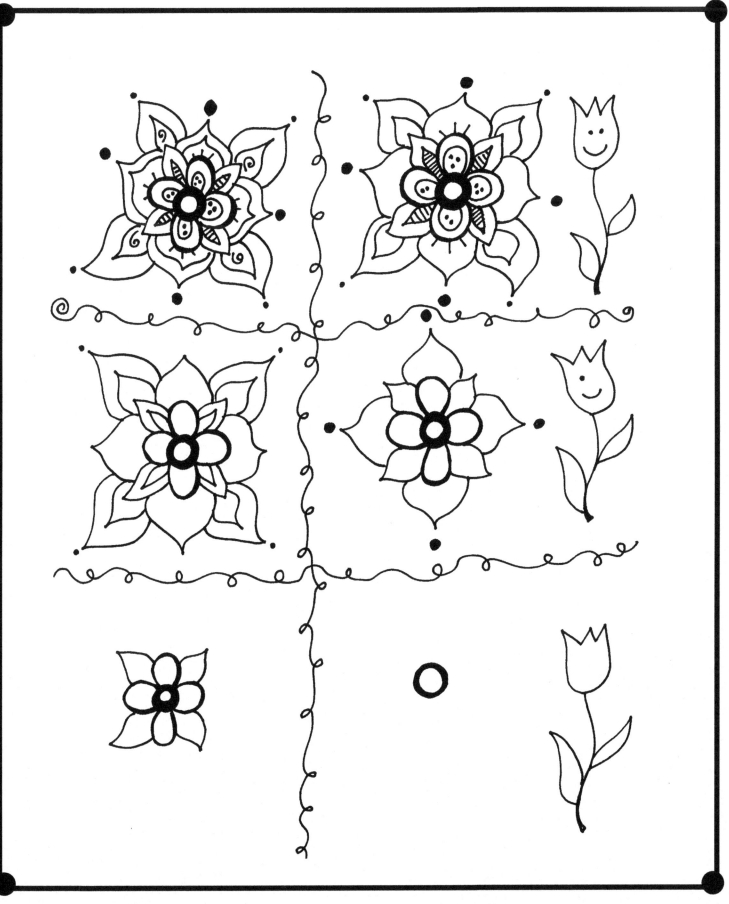

Name:_____ Date:_____

© 2011 all rights reserved. The Thinking Tree, LLC

Name:_____ Date:_____

© 2011 all rights reserved. The Thinking Tree, LLC

Name:_____ **Date:**_____

© 2011 all rights reserved. The Thinking Tree, LLC

Name:_____ Date:_____

© 2011 all rights reserved. The Thinking Tree, LLC

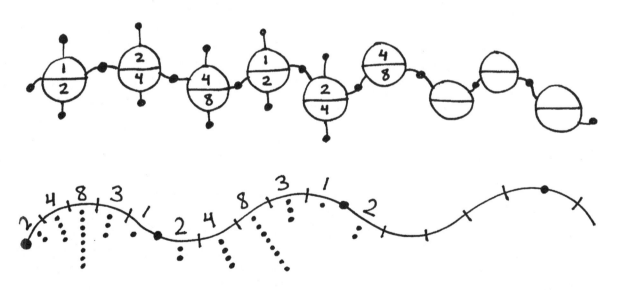

Name:_____ Date:_____

© 2011 all rights reserved. The Thinking Tree, LLC

Name:_____ Date:_____

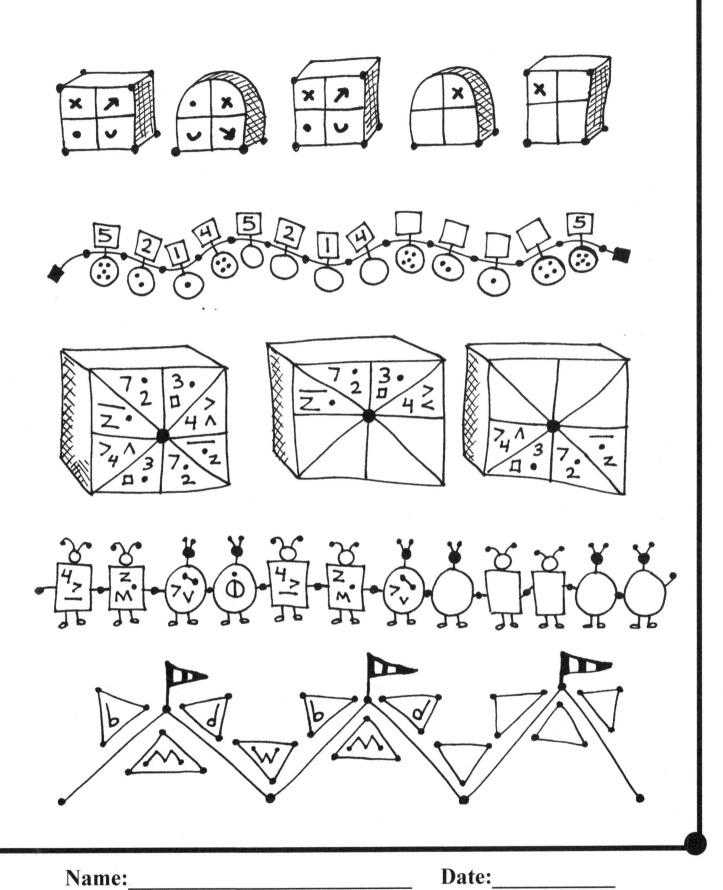

Name:_____ Date:_____

© 2011 all rights reserved. The Thinking Tree, LLC

Name:_____ Date:_____

© 2011 all rights reserved. The Thinking Tree, LLC

Name:_____ **Date:**_____

© 2011 all rights reserved. The Thinking Tree, LLC

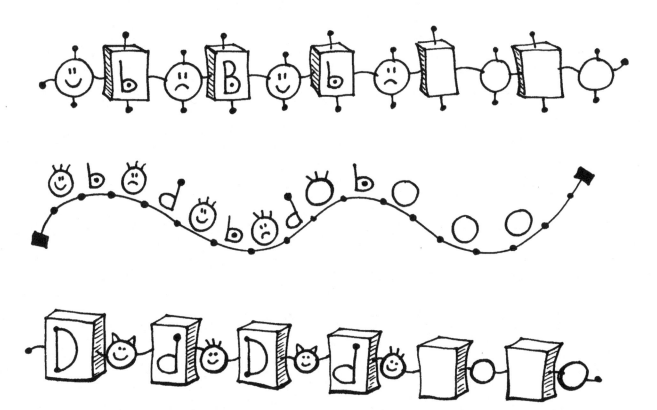

Name:_____ Date:_____

© 2011 all rights reserved. The Thinking Tree, LLC

Name:_____   Date:_____

© 2011 all rights reserved. The Thinking Tree, LLC

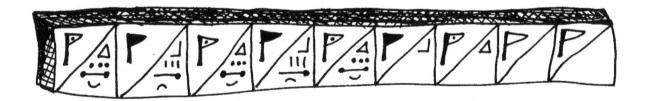

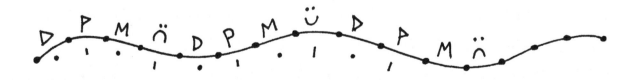

Name:_____ Date:_____

© 2011 all rights reserved. The Thinking Tree, LLC

Name:_____ **Date:**_____

Name:_____ Date:_____

© 2011 all rights reserved. The Thinking Tree, LLC

I.Q. Challenge

Certificate of Completion

Madeline 12
Name & Age

_____
Date of Completion

The Thinking TREE

Mom
Teacher

The Thinking TREE

www.DyslexiaGames.com

Copyright © 2011 the Thinking Tree, LLC
All rights reserved.

Created by: Sarah Janisse Brown

Made in the USA
Coppell, TX
20 November 2021